Summer and Winter

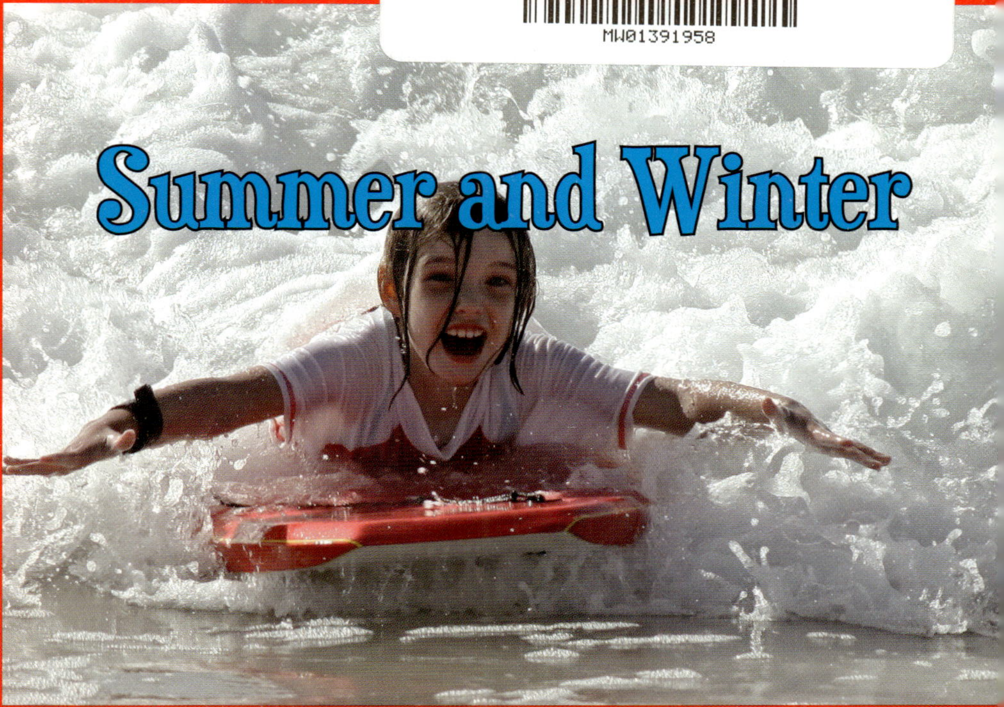

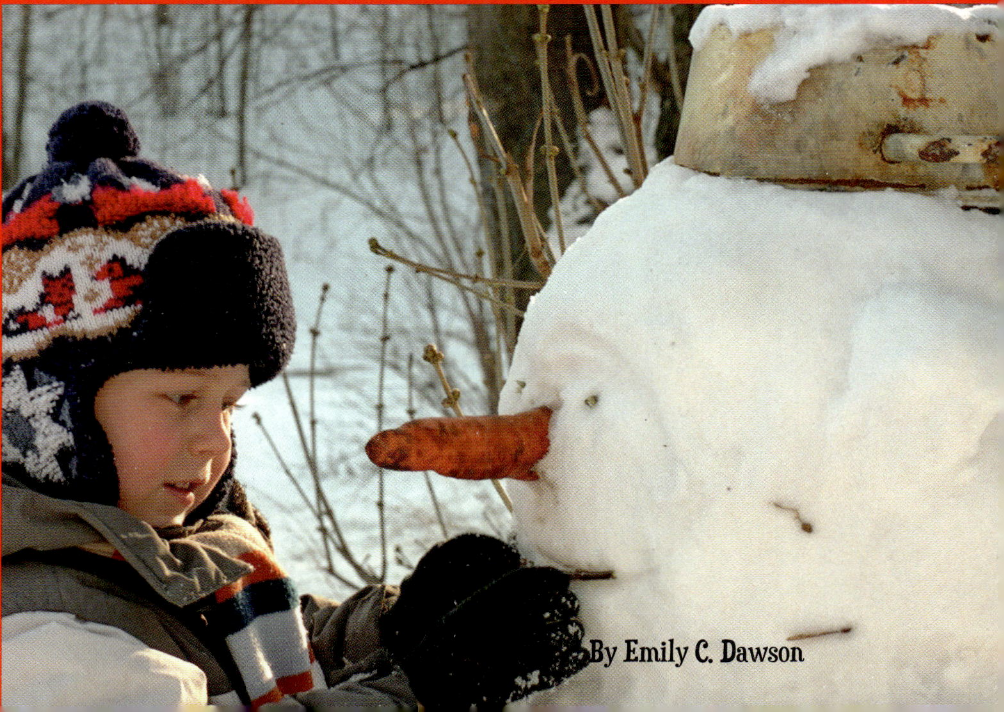

By Emily C. Dawson

RiverStream Readers
Great Reading • Real Learning

Learn to Read
Frequent repetition of sentence structures, high frequency words, and familiar topics provide ample support for brand new readers. Approximately 100 words.

Read Independently
Repetition is mixed with varied sentence structures and 6 to 8 content words per book are introduced with photo labels and picture glossary supports. Approximately 150 words.

Read to Know More
These books feature a higher text load with additional nonfiction features such as more photos, timelines, and text divided into sections. Approximately 250 words.

Accelerated Reader methodology uses Level A instead of Pre 1. We have chosen to change it for ease of understanding by potential users.

Amicus Readers hardcover editions published by Amicus. P.O. Box 1329, Mankato, Minnesota 56002
www.amicuspublishing.us

U.S. publication copyright © 2012 Amicus. International copyright reserved in all countries. No part of this book may be reproduced in any form without written permission from the publisher.

Printed in the United States of America at Corporate Graphics, in North Mankato, Minnesota.

Series Editor Rebecca Glaser
Series Designer Christine Vanderbeek
Photo Researcher Heather Dreisbach

RiverStream Publishing reprinted by arrangement with Appleseed Editions Ltd.

Library of Congress Cataloging-in-Publication Data
Dawson, Emily C.
  Summer and winter / by Emily C. Dawson.
    p. cm. – (Amicus Readers. Let's compare)
  Includes index.
  Summary: "Compares and contrasts summer and winter weather and activities you can do in each season. Includes comprehension activity"–Provided by publisher.
  ISBN 978-1-60753-003-9 (library binding)
  1. Summer–Juvenile literature. 2. Winter–Juvenile literature. I. Title.
  QB637.6.R87 2012
  508.2–dc22
                                    2010041757

Photo Credits
Susan Stewart/iStockphoto, Cover-top; Mike Kiev/iStockphoto, Cover-bottom; Bronwyn8, 4t, 21m; Jorn Georg Tomter/Getty Images, 4b, 22bl; Adam Crowley, 6, 22tl; Jakob Fridholm/Getty Images, 8; Alexander Crispin/Getty Images, 10, 21b; Jose Luis Pelaez/Getty Images, 12; Michael Jonsson/Getty Images, 14, 20t; Pictorium/Alamy, 16; Simon Wilkinson/Getty Images, 18, 22mr; Nathan Allred|Dreamstime.com, 20b; Maksym Gorpenyuk|Dreamstime.com, 21t; Echo/Getty Images, 21b; Ann Marie Kurtz/iStockphoto, 22ml; Michel de Nijs/iStockphoto, 22tr; Wavebreakmedia Ltd|Dreamstime.com, 22br

1 2 3 4 5 CG 15 14 13 12
RiverStream Publishing—Corporate Graphics, Mankato, MN—112012—1002CGF12

Table of Contents

Summer and Winter
5

Picture Glossary
20

Let's Compare Summer and Winter
22

Ideas for Parents and Teachers
23

Index
24

Web Sites
24

summer

Let's Compare!

winter

Let's compare summer and winter.

What can you do in each season?

summer

Summer has the warmest weather. Lani goes surfing. She wears sunscreen so she does not get a sunburn.

winter

Winter has the coldest weather. Amy puts on a hat and mittens. Then she makes a snow fort.

Let's Compare!

summer

It rains in summer.
May walks to
her friend's house
in the rain.

Let's Compare!

winter

It snows in winter. Sam and Iva go sledding. Then they drink hot chocolate.

summer

14

Summer days are longer. Jen hula hoops outside after supper.

winter

Winter days are shorter. Levi skis in the afternoon before the sun goes down.

Let's Compare!

18

What do you like to do in summer or winter?

Let's Compare!
Picture Glossary

hula hoop →
to twirl a large plastic hoop around your body

← **season**
one of the four natural parts of the year—spring, summer, fall, and winter

sledding →
riding down a snowy hill on a flat object called a sled

← skiing
gliding over snow on long, narrow runners called skis that are attached to your feet

surf →
to ride on breaking waves using a surfboard

← weather
what the outside air is like, such as hot or cold, rainy or windy

Summer and Winter

Look at the photos.
1. Which things do you do in summer?
2. Which things do you do in winter?
3. Which things can you do any time of the year?

Ideas for Parents and Teachers

Books 1 through 5 in the RiverStream Readers Level Pre 1 Series give children the opportunity to compare familiar concepts with lots of reading support. Repetitive sentence structures, high frequency words, and photo labels provide support for new readers. In each book, the picture glossary defines new vocabulary and the activity page reinforces compare and contrast techniques.

Before Reading
- Ask the child about the difference between summer and winter. Ask: What things do we do outside in summer? What things do we do outside in winter?
- Discuss the cover photos. What do these photos tell them?
- Look at the picture glossary together. Ask the child to sort the clothes into a summer group and a winter group.

Read the Book
- "Walk" through the book and look at the photos. Ask questions or let the child ask questions about the photos.
- Read the book to the child, or have him or her read independently.
- Show the child how to refer to the picture glossary and read the photo labels to understand the full meaning.

After Reading
- Do the activity on page 22 with the child.
- Prompt the child to think more, asking questions such as What are summer and winter like where we live? What do we do in each season?

Index

days   15, 17
hat   9
hot chocolate   13
hula hoop   15
mittens   9
rain   11
skiing   17
sledding   13
snow   13
snow fort   9
summer   5, 7, 11, 15, 19
sunburn   7
sunscreen   7
surfing   7
weather   7, 9, 11, 13
winter   5, 9, 13, 17, 19

Web Sites

The Seasons Activities at Enchanted Learning
http://www.enchantedlearning.com/themes/seasons.shtml

The Weather Channel for Kids
http://www.theweatherchannelkids.com/

Weather Wiz Kids
http://www.weatherwizkids.com/